THE LIFE AND TIMES

OF

𝕾aint 𝕬ldhelm,

FIRST BISHOP OF SHERBORNE, A.D. 705-709.

BY THE

REV. W. H. JONES, M.A., F.S.A.,

Prebendary of Sarum and Vicar of Bradford-on-Avon.

BATH:

WILLIAM LEWIS, "THE BATH HERALD" OFFICE, NORTH GATE.

1878.

THE LIFE AND TIMES

OF

SAINT ALDHELM.

MORE than eleven hundred years have passed away since the holy man, of whose life and labours we are about to give an account, lived and died. To very many of our readers his name will probably be almost unknown. And yet his work—that great work which with such faithfulness and self-denial he wrought for his Master—remains still. Certainly to none were our ancestors, who lived in what we now call the West of England, and which in their days formed part of the Kingdom of Wessex, more indebted for the blessings of Christianity, than to St. Aldhelm.

It is not of course meant to assert that Aldhelm was the very first who proclaimed the message of the Gospel in the western parts of our country. There is little doubt as to our British forefathers having received the "good news" within a comparatively short time of our blessed Lord's Ascension into heaven; and there are not a few who have thought that it was one of the Apostles who came hither as the first herald of the Gospel of Peace. For more than a century before the Romans quitted our island—which they did shortly after A.D. 400—the religion of the Empire was Christian. No very trustworthy records remain, and the details given to us respecting individual Bishops are often apocryphal; still there is no doubt of there having been a British Church with a native Episcopate flourishing here. But when our English ancestors first effected a settlement in this country, that is during the latter part of the fifth century, they were heathens, and such they continued for well-nigh two hundred years afterwards. During that long dark night of heathendom, they not only trampled upon, but refused to hear, the despised Briton, when he would fain have won them from the worship of idols to the service of the one living and true God; a fact that may in part excuse the British Bishops from the censure passed on them by Beda, that they never attempted the conversion of their heathen conquerors. In truth, it is to be feared that the heathenism of the latter had well-nigh obliterated all traces of the true faith, and that the mass of the inhabitants, in the middle of the seventh century, were practically strangers to the religion of Christ Jesus.

It was at this time, about the year A.D. 634, that a missionary Bishop, by name Birinus, came among the West Saxons to preach the Word of God. The first visit of this "Apostle of Wessex," as he has been rightly called, to our shores, is thus briefly related in the Anglo-Saxon Chronicle: —"A:D. 634. This year Bishop Birinus first preached baptism to the West Saxons under King Cynegils."—This date is, in several respects, an interesting and important one. Forty years had now passed since the commencement of Augustine's mission in England. During that comparatively long period, neither by Augustine, nor by any of his successors in the see of Canterbury, had the conversion of the West Saxons been attempted. It would seem to have been almost a tacit rebuke to them for wasting their energies in vain disputes with the Celtic Bishops whom they found in the country, and who refused to acknowledge their authority, on such trifling matters as the tonsure and the right day of observing Easter, that apparently without any communication with Honorius, then Archbishop of Canterbury, but nevertheless with the direct sanction of the Pope himself, Birinus came among the West Saxons, then "most confirmed Pagans."[1]   At all events the fact is clear, that for the *first* introduction of Christianity among the West Saxons, nothing is owing to Augustine or his immediate successors.

It was about the time when Birinus came to England—though we know for certain neither the year nor place—that Aldhelm was born. It was an eventful period in our country's history. Great success followed the efforts of the Missionary Bishop. Within a year of the commencement of his mission he was successful in converting King Cynegils to the Christian faith, and shortly afterwards other members of the king's family and many of his subjects made a like profession. He was the means moreover of permanently establishing Christianity in Wessex, by founding a bishopric, the seat of which was first at Dorchester in Oxfordshire, and afterwards at Winchester, from which, as a centre, he and those who succeeded him strove earnestly to extend the knowledge of the true faith.

---

[1] The expression used by Beda is "paganissimos." He says of Birinus that he was consecrated at Genoa, as a Bishop, by Asterius, Archbishop of Milan.   Pagi, in his annotations on Baronius (An. 635, § 3) says that he was not appointed to any *particular see*—in fact, he was a Missionary Bishop.—Bed. Eccles. Hist. III. 7.

Separated as we are from the times of which we are writing by a gulf of well-nigh 1200 years, it is hardly wonderful that we should find it difficult to give what might be deemed a really trustworthy account of Aldhelm's history. The notices concerning him in the writings of his contemporary Beda are but few and scanty, and the sketch of his life by Alfred the Great, which, as we infer from some remarks of William of Malmesbury, once existed, has long since perished.

The principal biography that is left to us was not written till four hundred years after his death, and its author was a monk of the Abbey, of which for a long time Aldhelm was the superior, and, as some say, the founder. The honour of the society seemed involved in exalting the fame of its Abbot, and so the story of his life abounds in fulsome eulogy, and a long detail of presumed miracles which the credulity of the age too willingly accepted as real. In truth, legend and fact are so strangely interwoven in the writings of the early monastic chroniclers, that it is difficult, and, at this distance of time, hopeless to attempt to disentangle them.

Aldhelm was of royal lineage. His father's name was Kenten, a near kinsman of Ine, who, in A.D. 688, became king of Wessex. According to

William of Malmesbury[1] he was first educated by
Hadrian, Abbot of St. Augustine's monastery at
Canterbury, but there are expressions in a charter[2]
relating to the foundation of the Abbey of Malmesbury that seem to imply that from early infancy
he was brought up there. At all events he soon
became a member of that religious house, and his
principal instructor appears to have been Maildulf,
a Scot, or perhaps Irish hermit who settled there
in the early part of the seventh century.

The history of Aldhelm is so intertwined with
that of the Abbey at Malmesbury, that it will be
necessary to give some brief account of that ancient
religious house.

Leland, in his Collectanea, deriving his infor-
mation from some old manuscripts which he saw
at Malmesbury, supplies us with some extracts
which throw a glimmer of light on its history in
remote times. " Some people say," are his words,
"that there was a house of Nuns close by the
castle of Ingelbourne, in a certain hamlet called
Ilanburgh, by the Saxons termed Burghton. They

---

[1] Gesta Pontif. (Rolls Series) p. 333.
[2] See Kemble's Cod. Dipl. No. 11. Bishop Leotherius (Hlothere) thus speaks of Aldhelm's early association with Malmesbury,
"in quo videlicet loco a primo ævo infantiæ .... et in gremio
sanctæ matris ecclesiæ nutritus vitam duxit"

were guilty of incontinence with the soldiers of
the castle and so were all expelled. They were
under the direction of Dinoth, Abbot of the famous
monastery of Bangor, who numbered some 2,000
monks in different places that looked up to him as
their superior."[1] The place referred to still bears
the name of Burton, and is close by Malmesbury.
The time that is alluded to would be about the
close of the sixth century. There may be some
truth as to the existence of this early religious
house, and it is only too probable that its inmates
were dispersed and their buildings destroyed by
the ruthless Saxons, who in their heathendom
burnt alike the churches and dwellings of the
British Christians. For it is remarkable, that, of
the numberless Roman villas and towns of which
the foundations have been discovered in all parts
of England, nearly every one bears marks of
having been destroyed by violence rather than by
time; fire apparently in most cases having been
the agent of destruction.[2]

It was no long time after the suppression of
this early British monastery, that Providence
guided the steps of Maildulf, the hermit, of whom
we have spoken, to this same spot. He was struck

[1] Leland, Collectanea, II. 304.
[2] See Parker's Introd. to Gothic Architecture, p. 10.

with the similarity of the wild wood-land to his own native country, and its suitableness for the retired life which he wished to lead. He asked permission to build himself a small dwelling, or, as we may say, a "cell," under Caer-Bladon, *i. e.* the castle on the Bladon, the name then given to the river flowing by Malmesbury which is now called the Avon. He was very poor, and so, as his learning was great for those days, he established a school for his maintenance, and amongst his scholars in due time was Aldhelm, a near relation, as we have seen, of King Ine.

By degrees Maildulf formed his scholars into a small society, and this was the real foundation of the great Abbey of Malmesbury, so famous in after times. In truth, his "monastery," if such indeed we call it, was after all but a voluntary association or brotherhood, hardly subject to rules, and held together by similarity of views and feelings among those who became members of it and by a common reverence for their teacher. And a very important end was served by Maildulf's brotherhood—it became in reality a missionary settlement or centre, from which the blessings of Christianity were conveyed to the surrounding population, as yet mostly heathen. Indeed the word "monastery," for some centuries after the time of which we are writing, frequently meant only a church with three or four priests attached to it. And no doubt many of the early monasteries had in the first instance very much the character of Moravian settlements, or of those stations established in the South of Africa by the late Bishop of Cape Town, or of those missionary brotherhoods which have been warmly advocated as a means, especially needed in India, for the propagation of the truth. They were in earliest days lay institutions connected with the Church, a few of the inmates of which were ordained, though they formed the exception rather than the rule. And very instrumental they were in bringing the people at large under the sway of the Gospel, when, possessors of lands, their occupants became themselves cultivators of the soil, and could speak in terms of equality and brotherly love to those slaves whom they had set at liberty, and teach them to serve Him " Whose service is perfect freedom."

This early training under Maildulf well prepared Aldhelm for the work to which he afterwards devoted himself. A few of the early years of his life were thus spent, and then he is said to have travelled in Gaul and Italy, and to have

studied in various schools of learning. On his
return to England, he sought instruction in Kent,
under Hadrian, an African by nation, and originally a monk of the Niridan monastery, situated
near Monte Cassino, in the kingdom of Naples.
Pope Vitalian, to whom the kings of Kent and
Northumbria agreed, under the peculiar circumstances of the times—especially with regard to
the angry disputes between the ancient British
Church and that planted by Augustine—to leave
the selection, had chosen this same Hadrian
for the see of Canterbury. Hadrian, though a
learned man, felt that something more was required for that high and responsible office, and so,
declining it for himself, had recommended Theodore, a native of Tarsus in Cilicia, as the man
whose practical talents and administrative ability
marked him out as eminently fitted for the post.
With true generosity he consented to accompany
the new Archbishop to England: and, when settled
at Canterbury, he established a school of theology,
in which the clergy were especially trained in a
knowledge of those things which it was their
mission to make known to others. William of
Malmesbury, in the florid language of his day
describes Hadrian as "a fountain of letters and a

river of arts." Together with Archbishop Theodore, he worked zealously and harmoniously in the
promotion of the great object on which each had
set his heart. "They regarded," it has been well
said,[1] " civilization as the handmaid of Christianity,
and of civilization they knew that learning is the
parent. They found the English people eager to
be instructed, and appetent of knowledge. They
gathered round them a crowd of disciples, and, as
Beda says, there daily flowed from them the
streams of knowledge to water the hearts of their
hearers. Through their influence, all the larger
and better monasteries were converted into schools
of learning, in which the laity as well as the
clergy imbibed a respect for literature, and, in
many instances, a love of it. In the time of
Beda, there were scholars of Theodore and Hadrian
who were as well versed in the Greek and Latin
languages as in their own."

Among the most distinguished of these was
certainly Aldhelm. More than once he seems to
have repaired to Kent, to receive instruction at
the " feet of Hadrian." As late as 680—some
years after he had become Abbot of the monastery
at Malmesbury in which his early youth was

[1] Hook's Lives of the Archbishops of Canterbury, I. 163.

passed—he signs himself, on one occasion, as a "scholar" or "disciple" of Archbishop Theodore.

It would appear that an attack of severe sickness compelled Aldhelm to leave Kent, and again to settle finally in his old home Malmesbury. A letter is still extant which he wrote three years after his return to his preceptor Hadrian, in which he describes the studies in which he was still occupied and the difficulties which he had encountered. His reputation for learning spread so extensively, that, not only the members of his society at Malmesbury looked up to him as their teacher, but scholars came to him from the distant regions of France and Scotland. One of his biographers tells us, that he could write and speak the Greek language like a native of Greece—that he excelled in Latin all scholars since the days of Virgil—that he was acquainted with Hebrew, and read the psalms and other parts of holy scripture in the original text. Some allowance must be made for the exaggerated estimates of admiring biographers, still there is no doubt that Aldhelm was one of the most learned and accomplished men of his time.

It must have been about the year 670, that Aldhelm was admitted into the honourable office of Abbot of the monastery of St. Peter and Paul at Malmesbury. It does not appear that Maildulf was dead; indeed, as far as we can obtain a clear account from the fragmentary and often conflicting statements of chroniclers, he would seem to have lived fourteen years after Aldhelm's formal appointment as Abbot, and generously to have submitted himself, as a member of the society, to the rule of his former disciple. William of Malmesbury tells us, in his Chronicle of the Kings of England (Book I. c. 2), that Hlothere, or, as he calls him, Leutherius (a name which modernised would assume the well-known form of Luther), Bishop of the West Saxons, whose see was at Dorchester, in Oxfordshire, "after long and due deliberation gave the monastery to Aldhelm, a monk of the same place, to be governed by him with the authority then possessed by Bishops." And then he gives a copy of the charter, which we also find in the Malmesbury Chartulary, by which Bishop Hlothere, bestows on "Aldhelm the priest, in order that he may lead a life according to strict rule, the portion of land called Mealdunesburg (=Malmesbury), in which place from his earliest childhood he had been instructed in the liberal arts, and passed his days nurtured in the bosom of the holy mother Church." The grant would seem to have included the whole site on which Malmesbury Abbey and its surrounding buildings afterwards rose.

A few years after the constitution of a regular monastery here its revenues were increased by endowments from various sources. The earliest benefactor was Ethelred, a king of Mercia, who, at the request of a kinsman, Cœnfrith Earl of Mercia, endowed it with lands at Long Newnton, and Charlton, "next Tetbury." Shortly afterwards, Cœdwealha, a king of Wessex, bestowed on Aldhelm an estate described as being "on either side of the wood called Kemele (= Kemble)," a gift which some seven years subsequently he considerably augmented. The original gift of Cœdwealha was certainly a remarkable one, inasmuch as the kings of Wessex had, after embracing Christianity, relapsed again into idolatry, and, at the very time when he was thus endowing Aldhelm's monastery, the king was professedly a heathen. Possibly the awe of a good man, and the secret conviction that Christianity, now openly professed in the kingdom of Mercia, was after all the true religion, may have moved him to this act. At all events in the year 688—the very time when he so considerably enlarged his gift to

Malmesbury,—the king went to Rome, accompanied by Aldhelm, and was there baptized by the Pope Sergius. We seem almost to infer from this circumstance, that the conversion of Cœdwealha was owing to the efforts of his earnest-minded kinsman, the Abbot of Malmesbury.

During his stay at Rome, which was only for a short time, Aldhelm seems to have been in constant communication with Pope Sergius, and to have been much honoured by him. He brought back with him a "bull," issued by the Pope, which conferred special privileges on his monastery. He was laden with valuable presents for the kings both of Wessex and Mercia. Amongst other things which he brought from Rome was a very valuable altar (or perhaps more correctly speaking an altar slab) of white marble, described by William of Malmesbury as "eighteen inches thick, four feet long, and some three palms" (*i. e.* from twelve to fourteen inches) "broad:"[1] this he gave, on his return home, to the church at Briwetune (Bruton), where it still remained in the twelfth century.

William of Malmesbury becomes almost eloquent when he describes the joy of the people on Aldhelm's returning safely from what in those days was a

[1] Gesta Pontificum (Rolls Series), p. 373.

tedious and perilous journey. A long procession formed of all classes met him on his arrival and welcomed him. Some, members of religious houses or of various orders of the Church, chanted hymns before him, or carried the "Holy Rood," or swung censers full of incense, as a symbol of their joy. The laity testified their welcome in other ways, by shoutings and dances. The kings, moreover, of Wessex and Mercia, Ine and Ethelred, shared in the common exultation, and a holy pact was formed between them, to the effect that even should differences arise between them and war ensue, the Abbey at Malmesbury, standing as it did in what was for a long time a kind of border-land of the two kingdoms, should be reverenced by them, and held sacred from injury. Substantial favours quickly followed, and estates at Somerford, Garsdon, and Rodbourne, were bestowed on his Abbey.

Aldhelm had succeeded to his office, as Abbot of Malmesbury, in most eventful times, and no doubt did his part in the great work that was going on, under Archbishop Theodore, in giving a permanent character to the Christianity of England. Previous labourers had done much towards this all-important end, and effects that might be deemed almost marvellous, did we not remember how many circum-

stances rendered the people willing to receive the
Gospel, followed their efforts. The ancient British
Church, crushed, as far as might be, by the heathen
Saxon, held forth, though with feeble hands, the
lamp of truth. The Christianity of the native Britons,
even in their state of subjection to their cruel op-
pressors, was still faithfully though often secretly
maintained. There is a vitality in the religion we
profess, so that, though it may seem well-nigh
extinguished at times by the hand of persecution,
from its smouldering smoke the flame soon bursts
forth again, when, in God's providence, the tyrant's
hand is loosed, or his heart is softened. So it
was once in Madagascar. "Cast down, but not
destroyed,"—such has often been a description of
the Christians there, when, as has been the case,
they have been forced to succumb to some cruel
edict, the object of which was to extirpate all
traces of the religion of Christ from the island.
But even then, as Bishop Ryan has told us, the
seed, though trampled under foot, lived all along
and germinated in secret, ready again to blossom
when favourable circumstances might favour its
development. So it was in our own country in
Anglo-Saxon times. Thousands of souls gathered,
in but a few years, within the fold of the Church

of Christ, showed clearly enough, that, when the sower came forth to sow his seed, the soil was already prepared for its reception.

Of Aldhelm's life, as Abbot of Malmesbury, there are not many trustworthy details preserved to us. Under his care and guidance his monastery soon acquired fame as a seat of piety and learning. It became moreover a centre of religious influence over all the surrounding country. The chroniclers are unanimous in bearing witness to Aldhelm's unceasing efforts to do good, and to his constant acts of painful self-denial, notwithstanding much weakness of body, that he might shew the example of a holy life to all who came under his rule.

One anecdote related concerning him, which William of Malmesbury professes to have obtained from the manual or note-book of King Alfred, is too characteristic to be omitted. Observing with pain that the country-people who came to hear divine service could with difficulty be persuaded to listen to the exhortations of the preacher, Aldhelm determined to seek to impress the truth of Christianity upon them in another way. He was a good musician as well as a poet, and so, watching the occasion, he stationed himself on the bridge over which the people had to pass, and, in the character

of a minstrel, recited and sang to them some popular
songs. A crowd of listeners soon collected round
him, and when he had gained their attention he
gradually introduced words of a more serious
character, till at last he succeeded in impressing
on their minds a true feeling of devotion. We all
know how much the Reformation was advanced in
this country and elsewhere by the use of singing
psalms, though few of us remember, that, in the
commencement of Christianity among our Saxon
forefathers, it was the same use which promoted the
knowledge of religion with them, the psalm itself
being frequently called by them the "harp-song."

But Aldhelm was diligent in other ways. At
Malmesbury he is said to have built two churches,
one within the monastery for the use of its
inmates, and another without its walls for the
towns-people or villagers. The former he erected
on the foundations of an old British church and
dedicated to St. Peter and St. Paul, in that age
the favourite saints of the Anglo-Saxons. He
wrote some Latin verses on the occasion of the
formal consecration of his church which are preserved to us by William of Malmesbury. We
may mention in passing that in like manner the
churches erected in the seventh century at Canter-

bury and Glastonbury, were built on the foundations or from the ruins of older churches. So too the churches of St. Paul's and Westminster were restorations by Mellitus, Bishop of London, of buildings which had been formerly consecrated by the Celtic bishops.

The Chroniclers also tell us of his generous zeal in building a church, near his own private estate, "not far from Wareham (in Dorset), where also Corfe Castle stands out in the sea[1]," the remains of which were still to be seen in the days of William of Malmesbury, and within the ruins of which, he adds, the shepherds of the district were wont to flee for shelter from storms. He is said also to have founded a church, dedicated to St. Peter, at Briwetune (Bruton) in Somerset.

In addition to these good works, Aldhelm is known to have founded two smaller monasteries and churches, at Frome and at Bradford-on-Avon respectively, which were, so to speak, dependencies on the larger Abbey of Malmesbury, and the inmates of which looked to him as their superior, and rendered him willing allegiance. Of these two subordinate monasteries William of Malmesbury speaks particularly. Writing at the latest,

[1] Gesta Pontificum (Rolls Series), p. 364.

about A.D. 1115, he says that at Frome, the church built by him, which had been dedicated to St. John Baptist, was still standing in his time. And he adds that at Bradford also, though the *monastery,* as was the case also at Frome, had perished, there still remained in his days " the little church,—he calls it *ecclesiola,*—which Aldhelm is said to have built and dedicated to St. Laurence [1]."

And most interesting it is to be able to add, that this *" little church "*—the work of Aldhelm at the very beginning of the eighth century, within, that is, some *seventy years* of the first preaching of the Gospel to the West Saxons by St. Birinus,—is *still in existence.* After having been desecrated and forgotten for centuries—concealed from view by factories, or stables, built up against it—it has once more been brought to light, and literally dug out of the earth, which in the course of years had accumulated in some places to the height of six feet above the foundations.

A few words may not be deemed out of place respecting this perfectly *unique* and most interesting church, which it was the privilege of the writer to discover some eighteen years ago.

As the building appears now, it consists of a

[1] Gesta Pontificum (Rolls Series), p. 346.

chancel, a nave, and a porch on the north side. A minute examination however of the wall on the south side, against which a modern house has been erected, shews that at one time there was on that side also a building of much the same dimensions as the present porch, so that the little church was cruciform originally. The accompanying wood-cut shows its ground plan as it is at the present time.

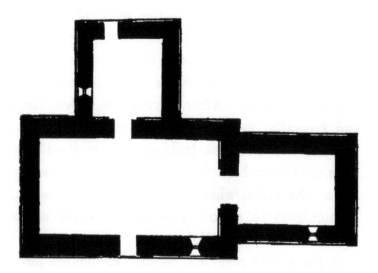

A view, shewing the appearance of the "little church" from the south-east, is given as a frontis-piece. It may be stated among its peculiarities, that the workmanship is of a very rude description,

and that the arcading, as represented in that en-
graving, is not at all constructive, but simply
surface decoration; in fact, the walls seem to have
been built at first plain, with the bands or
string-courses alone projecting, the panels and
ornamentation being afterwards formed in them.
Moreover, the great height of the building, in
comparison with its length and breadth, is most
remarkable, reminding us of the drawings in
manuscripts of the eighth and following centuries,
which we have sometimes thought were out of
proportion, but which this example proves were
very probably true enough in this respect [1].

Another striking feature in this church is the
opening from the chancel into the nave, which is
indeed rather a doorway than what we usually
mean by a chancel arch, being only about three feet
wide and about ten feet high; but in other very
early churches which remain, the opening from the
nave to the chancel is very small, and adapted to
the Eastern rather than the Western ritual.

Over this arch, some eight feet above it, imbedded
in the wall, are two stone figures of angels, one on
either side.

[1] The following are the dimensions of this "little church."
The Nave is about 24 feet 2 inches by 13 feet 2 inches, and 25 feet
5 inches high; the Chancel 13 feet 2 inches by 10 feet, and 18 feet
4 inches high; the Porch 9 feet 11 inches by 10 feet 5 inches and
15 feet 6 inches high.

These figures, which, if not coeval with the building itself, are certainly as early as the tenth century, are

executed in a kind of low relief: the angels have their wings expanded, around their heads is the *nimbus*, and over an arm each holds what is conjectured to represent a napkin. It is conceived that originally there was a central figure of our Blessed Lord upon the cross. There is to be seen still in the curious though sadly mutilated sculpture in the church of Headbourne Worthy [1], near Winchester (a building, the principal portion of which is of the date of the tenth century), a design which seems to warrant such a conjecture.

[1] See a drawing of this church, showing this rood with the two attendant figures of St. Mary and St. John, in the Journal of the Archæological Association (Winchester Volume), p. 412.

An effort has been made, within the last three years, to recover and preserve this precious relic of early Christianity, and happily with success. The "little church" has been purchased, in fragments, from its owners, for the Nave belonged to one proprietor and the Chancel to another, at an expense of some £560, which has been met by voluntary contributions, and conveyed to trustees with a view to its permanent preservation for the time to come.

It is hoped that the offerings of English Churchmen will soon enable the trustees to commence the work of reparation. At present they are quite at a *standstill*, all funds hitherto supplied to them having been required for the purchase and its attendant expenses. About £1,000 are still wanted for the completion of the work. Still they are sanguine that before long that work may be commenced, and that in this "little church," rescued from the desecration of so many hundred years, may once more be heard the voice of prayer and praise[1].

[1] Among the trustees of this Saxon Church in virtue of their office, are the Archdeacon of Wilts and the Vicar of Bradford-on-Avon for the time being. The latter is Treasurer of the Fund raised for its reparation, and will most thankfully receive any contribution, even though small, for this good object.

Returning now to the regular course of our narrative, we must revert for a moment or two to Birinus, and the work which he accomplished as the first " messenger of peace" to the West Saxons.

The bishopric which he founded, as we have seen, at Dorchester (in Oxfordshire), was afterwards transferred to Winchester. He was succeeded in his episcopate by Ægelbyrht, Wina, Hlothere, and Headda, and during the seventy years that these holy men laboured, one after another, much progress was made in bringing the semi-heathen inhabitants of Wessex to the knowledge of the truth.

But self-denying efforts were being made in the East, as well as in the West, of England. We have already made allusion to the work that was going on in England under Archbishop Theodore. That "grand old man," as the Dean of Chichester rightly calls him, who was well-nigh threescore years and ten before he entered upon his high office, effected a marvellous change within the twenty-two years during which he held the see of Canterbury. It is no part of our present subject to dwell on Theodore's efforts, except so far as they paved the way for Aldhelm, who was afterwards

the means to a great extent of conciliating the ancient British Church, that still assumed a hostile attitude towards that established by Augustine. And these cannot be better described than in the words of the Dean of Chichester, in his Lives of the Archbishops of Canterbury (I. 192):—
"Hitherto the Church in England, whether we have regard to Celtic churches, or to those connected with the Canterbury mission after the expulsion of the British bishops, was simply a great station for missionary operations. Sometimes on horseback, but oftener on foot, the missionary would go forth from his monastery to the towns in the plain, whither the people would flock to hear the Word and to receive the Sacraments. At other times he would be absent for whole weeks, having scaled the craggy mountain, and having penetrated the recesses occupied by the bandit and the outlaw, where none but he could dare approach, seeking to allure the wild people by his preaching and example to heavenly employments. The missionaries only required a few houses besides the church, and *in the church,* when the houses were full from an unexpected return of the missionaries, they would direct the straw to be strewn for their beds. They were

frequently visited by the wealthy, but only shared with them their simple fare, and made no extra provision for their entertainment; and if the great men of the world, on departing, left them donations in money, it was spent in making provision for the poor."

But all the clergy were not engaged in missionary labour. From the migratory character of their courts, the princes were accustomed to select certain of the clergy to accompany them for the performance of the services of the Church: and the thanes, or nobles, soon followed their examples, and appointed their private chaplains. On this foundation Theodore erected his parochial system. He perceived that Christianity, if it was to be rooted in the land, required more than the occasional delivery of a sermon and the administration of sacraments; he recognized the superintending duties of a pastor who should gather the sheep in one fold. He persuaded the thanes and landed proprietors to place a church in the centre of their estates, and so to secure a constant intercourse between the minister of the Gospel, the inmates of the castle, and the serfs. By degrees he laid the foundation of what we now call the parochial system; and converted what had before been but a missionary station into a permanently established church. The Saxon Chronicle notices his death under the year 690 with this brief but significant remark: " Before this, the Bishops had been Romans; from this time they were English,"—in fact, a native church, henceforth supplied by a native ministry, had become a part of the constitution of the country.

Brihtwald, the first native Archbishop, was consecrated to the see of Canterbury at Lyons in 693. He was of royal lineage, being related to Ethelred the Mercian king. His accession as Archbishop was followed by marked results as regarded the real progress of Christianity; and these were owing in no small degree to the influence and efforts of Aldhelm.

There was, as we are all aware, a long continued and bitter enmity existing between the Celtic churches and those which recognized the authority of the successors of Augustine at Canterbury. Very hard things have been often said of the early British Christians, and they have been accused of grudging the blessings of the Gospel to the Anglo-Saxons. Apparently there would seem to have been a fixed determination among them not to attempt the conversion of those who had conquered

them, and held them in subjection. Still we must
not be too severe on them, for the wrongs they
had received had been great. This does not of
course justify their conduct; still one cannot but
feel that this difficulty arose in part from the
contemptuous unwillingness on the part of the
conquering Englishman to listen to the preaching
of the despised and persecuted Briton. The fierce-
ness of the hatred that existed between them
rendered, for a time, all union impossible. Even
trivial matters, such as the right day for observing
Easter, and a peculiar mode of tonsure, were exaggerated into importance, and raised up as barriers
against all communion between the two Churches.
The determination of the British Bishops, which
was not to be broken by the imperious demands of
Augustine, had hitherto also refused to yield to
the more polite diplomacy of Theodore.

But a change was coming over the scene. At
the very commencement of his archiepiscopate,
Brihtwald had the gratification of seeing a code
of laws promulgated by King Ine, in which
Christianity was fully acknowledged as the basis
of all moral and social obligation; and we can
hardly doubt that to this important step the king
was urged by his friend and kinsman Aldhelm.

Immediately afterwards a desire for union and reconciliation was evinced by the British bishops who expressed their readiness to yield on the question of Easter. In Cornwall the bishops retained the old usage, but they were met by Brihtwald in a truly Christian spirit. He employed Aldhelm to act the part of mediator between them, and, amongst other efforts, to write a letter to Gerent, prince of Cornwall—whom he addresses as the " glorious lord of the Western realm" (the letter is still extant) ; and, by this means, we are told, many of their objections were removed. Peace was soon afterwards cemented between the two Churches;—the consequence of the mild and fatherly rule of Brihtwald, and the wise and charitable counsels of Aldhelm.

No doubt there were many abuses and corruptions even in this early age of the Church. But though a tendency to superstition prevailed, no one can read the account of the doings of the latter part of the seventh century, without seeing that it was a turning point in the history of the Church of this country, and allowing that there must have been real progress in vital Christianity, as evidenced by the wonderful change which took place in the whole state of society. The Dean of Chichester well says, in reference to this change—"War, which had formerly been the pastime of the great, and the chief employment of a people eager of plunder, was now regarded as a cruel necessity, from the excitement of which kings and princes were eager to escape. A desire to enjoy the pleasures of retirement and the spiritual enthusiasm of the contemplation of life became a passion. Nobles left their halls and the mead-bench, queens their palaces, and kings the pomp and circumstance of war, when the duties of the royal vocation could be performed by younger men, and the public welfare no longer demanded their services. By retirement, at that period of our history, was meant a monastic retreat; but we know from Beda that it was not necessary for every one who at this period joined a monastery to bind himself to be a monk for ever, or even to seclude himself from society." Such an altered state of things attests the reality of the work that had been going on for some years previously. Making every allowance for wild enthusiasm, a flame easily kindled and as easily extinguished, we must admit that in the days of Brihtwald there was what in these latter times men would not scruple to call a general revival of religion. The prevalent feeling of the age was the love of piety, and to this result no one contributed more effectually than the good Abbot of Malmesbury.

It was not wonderful that when the necessities of the Church required for its due superintendence an increase in the number of its bishops, such a man as Aldhelm should have been marked out as eminently fitted for this high office. At the commencement of the eighth century there was indeed in the see of Winchester all that is now contained in the counties of Hampshire, Surrey, Wilts, Bucks, Dorset, Somerset, and (nominally at least) Devon and Cornwall. The two last-named counties were virtually in the hands of the British, and were called West Wales. Moreover there were very many Britons in the western parts of Wessex—that is in Somerset and Dorset. The charge of so enormous a diocese was far beyond the powers of a single bishop. Indeed his work must have been chiefly that of a missionary, travelling about from place to place, seeking to bring the heathen or semi-Christianized inhabitants to a profession of the faith.

Hence when by the decease of Headda, in 705, the see of Winchester became vacant, it was determined by Ine, then King of Wessex, that there should be two bishops instead of one, pre-

.siding respectively over its Eastern and Western portions. The see of the latter was fixed at Sherborne in Dorset, and Aldhelm was appointed as the first Bishop. He was consecrated to his high office by his friend, and, as some will have it, his kinsman Archbishop Brihtwald.

It is not very easy to define accurately the .precise limits of Aldhelm's diocese. In these early days, before the boundaries of what we now call counties were settled, there would seem to have been a large forest—it was called Sel-wood, i.e. *great wood*—which stretched from north to south, through a good portion of the western portion of Wiltshire. So when they came to form two dioceses, this large forest was fixed upon as a convenient border-line between them. Thus Aldhelm's diocese was described as all "west of Selwood;"—one chronicler indeed calls it Selwood-shire. So that, as without doubt this great forest stretched eastward a considerable way, there can be no doubt that Bradford-on-Avon, Malmesbury, Bishop-strow, and many other places in Wilts, besides the whole of Somerset and Dorset, were comprised in it.

It was with great misgiving as to his own powers, that Aldhelm consented to undertake the charge of this newly-constituted diocese. In truth he at the first declined it, pleading his age and infirmities, for he was now seventy years old and of by no means vigorous health, as a reason why the lot should fall on some one else. But these objections were happily over-ruled, and, to use the chronicler's words, "the Bishops welcomed him as a colleague, the clergy as a father, the laity as a friend." It was no slight charge which the "good Aldhelm" thus entered upon, for, to say nothing of its immense extent, a large portion of it was still almost unchristianized. Among the subjects of King Ine must have been many who had worshipped Thor and Woden in their youth—many who perhaps secretly cherished the ancient worship in their hearts.

As soon as Aldhelm entered upon the duties of his new office he expressed a wish to retire from that which he had now for many years held as Abbot of the monastery at Malmesbury, involving, as it did, the superintendence also of the branch societies which, as we have seen, he had established at Bradford and Frome. But the members of the various households unanimously urged him, and ultimately prevailed on him, to permit them still to look up to him as their superior. It speaks much for the love and respect with which they regarded the good Bishop.

Aldhelm held the see of Sherborne only for the short space of four years. His biographer, William of Malmesbury, dwells lovingly on the earnestness and self-denial of the holy Bishop in carrying out the duties of his high office. He travelled about from place to place, as one of the most devoted of missionaries, nearly always on foot, with his "ashen-stock" to help him forward, and, wherever he had the opportunity, preaching the Gospel to the people, and planting the Church in their midst. The chronicler indeed tells us, that, when he halted, he planted his "ashen-stock" in the ground, and that from such spots *trees* afterwards sprung forth; and he adds, that the name "Bishopstrow," which he explains as meaning "Bishop's-tree," was thus called from having been the scene of one of the Bishop's ministrations. We smile at the credulity of the mediæval chronicler; but after all, there is, so to speak, some fragment, nay, more than a fragment, of truth, underlying his explanation. He did not know, perchance, that the old Anglo-Saxon word "treow" meant not only "tree" but also a "cross," as it is employed, indeed, in our authorized version of the Bible, in Acts v. 30: "Whom they slew and hanged on a *tree*," and so

that the name *Biscopes-treow*[1], as it used to be
written, might fairly be interpreted as *Bishops-
cross*, the place where he literally planted the cross,
and preached to the people "the Word of Life."
Perhaps, like Augustine, he carried before him a
simple wooden cross, and held up before the people,
or fixed in the ground, this symbol of our faith,
whilst he proclaimed to them the truth of Christ
crucified. The very name at all events tells us of
the earnest labours of this holy man and true missionary, if it only bring before us the scene of his
labours, when, standing under some *tree* for shelter,
he preached to the people the Word of Life. And
there can be no doubt that Bishopstrow is a memo-
rial to the good Bishop, for the church is still dedicated to him. We may mention, in passing, that in
a somewhat similar way the memory of Felix, the first
Bishop of East Anglia, the see of which was fixed at
Dunwich, is still preserved in the name of Felix-stow,
a little village in the neighbourhood of Norwich.

It was whilst engaged in his sacred work, at no
great distance from Bishopstrow, of which we have
just spoken, that Aldhelm finished his earthly
course. It was near Doulting, a small village in

[1] In like manner the name Oswes-try means Oswald's-tree (or
cross), and is represented in Welsh by the name Croes-Oswallt.
Nicholas' Pedigree of the English People, p. 459.

Somerset, the Church of which is still dedicated to him, not far from Shepton Mallett, that he felt himself smitten with a mortal sickness. He straightway directed his attendants to carry him into the little wooden church, where he had himself ministered to the flock he had gathered around him as their shepherd; and there, looking steadfastly towards that sacred spot where they were wont to kneel to be partakers of the Holy Sacrament of the Body and Blood of Christ, peacefully breathed his soul into the hands of that great Shepherd and Bishop of Souls Who "loved him and gave Himself for him."

Under the direction of Ecgwin, Bishop of Worcester, the remains of the good Bishop were brought to Malmesbury, and there buried in the Chapel of St. Michael, which itself had been built by Aldhelm. Stone crosses were erected as memorials, at intervals, along the road by which they bore him to his burial. William of Malmesbury tells us that some of these remained in his days— that is, for some four hundred years after Aldhelm's decease. In the reign of King Edwy, the bones of Aldhelm, having been discovered and disinterred, were enshrined with much solemnity by Dunstan, Archbishop of Canterbury. And, according to Leland, though it is by no means easy to weave a consistent narrative out of the extracts which he gives us (*Collectanea*, II. 299), they seem to have been again removed by Osmund, Bishop of Sarum, his successor, as regards a considerable portion of his diocese, at the commencement of the twelfth century.

A place has been given to Aldhelm in the Roman calendar, and May 25th appointed as the day for his commemoration. Few certainly, from all we can learn respecting him, more fairly deserved to be had in grateful remembrance than the first bishop of Sherborne.

Aldhelm does not appear to have been a voluminous writer. Those works alone which give celebrity to his name were his " Ænigmata," and his two treatises on " Virginity." These are filled with Latinized Greek words, and with awkward expressions which render them obscure, and they abound with metaphor, often strained and unnatural, and in alliteration. Even William of Malmesbury felt compelled to offer an apology for Aldhelm's style, grounded on the corrupt taste of the age in which he lived.

There is, it may be mentioned, in the Lambeth Library, a very ancient copy of Aldhelm's work " De Virginitate" (Cod. 200 *f.* 68 b.), which competent judges have pronounced to be a work of the eighth century. An account of this manuscript is given in the Introduction to the Lambeth Catalogue, and in the same book in the frontispiece a *fac-simile* is engraved of the first leaf of the manuscript, which contains an illustration representing Aldhelm, in his episcopal chair, giving the book to an abbess and several attendant nuns.

Aldhelm claims to have been the first Englishman who wrote Latin poetry, and we have a few of his productions remaining to us. Of his Anglo-Saxon verses, which are said to have been much prized by King Alfred, none have come down to us. He is said also to have translated the Psalms of David into the vernacular tongue, but there is no authority for the opinion, too hastily adopted by Churton in his history of the "Early English Church," that the Anglo-Saxon version of them discovered in the Library at Paris, and edited by Thorpe, is to be attributed to him.

So lived and so died, working for his Master, even unto the end, the "Good Aldhelm," as the chroniclers love to call him. We may smile perhaps at the tales which a veneration for his memory has led them too readily to believe concerning presumed miracles wrought by him, but there can be no doubt of his having been from his youth upwards a man of

personal holiness and self-denial. Allusions are
more than once made by William of Malmesbury
to a *note-book* of King Alfred, who lived within 150
years of St. Aldhelm's decease, in which were
many notices concerning him. That note-book is
lost, but the entries alluded to show at all events
the estimation in which he was held by Alfred the
Great. And who knows but that the "good"
King himself, amid his wanderings, may have
come to Bradford-on-Avon, and there in the little
church, still so wonderfully preserved, founded by
Aldhelm himself, may have prayed earnestly to Al-
mighty God for help amid the troubles that at one
time oppressed him. Indeed, in the few writings
that are left to us, especially in extracts that
are given to us from his letters, we cannot fail to
see evidences of that earnest spirit that influenced
Aldhelm in his every act. No father could write
a more loving letter to a child, than one, preserved
by William of Malmesbury,[1] which was addressed
by him to Adilwald, a young but erring pupil.
He urges him by the love of Christ to resist
those worldly temptations which are proving so
dangerous a snare to him. "My beloved," are his
words, "remember what is written. Youth and
pleasure are vanity; 'for what shall it profit a

[1] See Gesta Pontif. (Rolls Series), p. 339.

man if he gain the whole world and lose his own soul?' Give thyself therefore now to divine readings, and ever watch in holy prayers." And in another letter, alluded to by the chronicler, he tells us simply yet beautifully, how these two means of grace especially bring us into communion with God;—"When I read the Word of God, then God is speaking to my soul; when I offer my prayers, then I am speaking to my God[1]."

But of course the especial view in which St. Aldhelm must be regarded, is that which brings out more distinctly the influence which he exercised for good on the times in which he lived. Of this certainly our narrative will have given abundant evidence. The kinsman of Ine, King of Wessex, and the friend also of the King of Mercia, Aldhelm had a power for good granted but to few, and how well he used it none can surely help acknowledging. Perhaps one of the greatest services he rendered to the progress of the true faith was when, as a peace-maker, yet with a firm adherence to his own convictions, he reconciled the differences that had for so many years existed between the ancient British Church and that of which Augustine in the east, and St. Birinus in the west, had been the first planters in

[1] Gesta Pontif. (Rolls Series) p. 357.

this country. In truth, he was one of those "of whom the world was not worthy," and was raised up by God as a special instrument for the advancement of His truth. As far at least as the kingdom of Wessex is concerned, his, without doubt, was the guiding hand that impressed upon it that character for good of which the evidences are so abundant. Few, it is conceived, will withhold from him the just meed of praise for having striven to the utmost to plant deeply and surely the true faith in his country. And making every allowance for those exaggerations with which the credulity of monkish writers have dwelt on the excellencies of his character, none who fairly consider his life and labours can deny his earnest piety, and his burning desire to promote peace and love among all who professed a common faith.

It would not be difficult, in several important particulars, to draw a parallel between Aldhelm and another holy man, who, many years afterwards, presided over a portion of the same district, as Bishop of Salisbury. Jewel, no less than Aldhelm, lived in troublous times, when a great struggle was being waged for the truth. Each Bishop according to his opportunity, and the special needs of his Church, became a valiant champion for its doctrine and its discipline. Each put his hand to the plough, and looked not back, nor let go his hold, till death loosened his grasp of it. The simple and touching story of Bishop Jewel's decease is well known,—how, when already, as he knew, stricken with a mortal malady, he preached his last sermon at Lacock, in accordance with his noble saying, "*Oportet Episcopum prædicantem mori* [1]"; how, bent with suffering, and against the expostulation of friends, he toiled on wearily to Monkton Farleigh, and there laid him down to die, praying humbly with almost his last breath, "Lord, now lettest Thou Thy servant depart in peace,—Lord, receive my spirit." Does it not seem almost a repetition, with a change of time and place, of the tale of Aldhelm, who, nine hundred years previously, under a like pressure of infirmities, was engaged to the very last in doing his Master's work,—whose lips were scarce closed in delivering his message of peace before they were murmuring calmly and trustfully his *Nunc Dimittis*, in that little wooden church at Doulting that gave a rude yet peaceful shelter to the dying Bishop. And who can doubt that each of these "noble workers for Christ" has received from Him, Who is the "great Shepherd and Bishop of our souls" that "crown of life" which He promises to all who are "faithful unto death."

[1] That is "It well becomes a Bishop to die preaching" (the Gospel).

Lightning Source UK Ltd.
Milton Keynes UK
UKHW020629220822
407644UK00005B/627